Beefy's Tune (Dean Blunt Edit)

Dhanveer Singh Brar

Published 2020 by the87press
The 87 Press LTD
87 Stonecot Hill
Sutton
Surrey
SM3 9HJ
www.the87press.co.uk

Beefy's Tune © Dhanveer Singh Brar 2020

The moral right of Dhanveer Singh Brar has been asserted in accordance with the Copyright, Designs and Patents Act 1988

ISBN: 978-1-8380698-1-0

Photograph: Edward George. Dub Housing 2013 - 2019
Design: Stanislava Stoilova [www.sdesign.graphics]

Preface

One of the things in motion at *the87press*, and a larger contemporary writing ecosystem, is an attention to experimental form and radical poetics which situates itself within a framework of radical inclusivity and alterity foregrounding the relationship between form and content. The open-access journal *darkmatter* has for many years been a proponent of cultural and postcolonial critique that had been at the forefront of innovative circulation in digital form forging discourse and networks across fractured space. The collaboration between the press and the journal enables an opportunity for critical writing that is given space to develop innovative styles that can circulate in the pockets of widening (counter)publics.

In developing the critical essay form we are particularly interested in a style that uses the cultural object as a cipher into larger questions within contemporary discourses. And in doing so, opening fields of inquisition across genre, form and so on, that might enable a certain level of creativity in writing that open avenues of thinking-to-come. The return to the book-form too suggests the need for an augmented materiality of affect and network. And yet by our focus on the essay-as-book here, we are signalling something of the need for incompleteness and unfinished-ness as resistances to some of the market and institutional imperatives within critical and creative work at our current moment.

Dhanveer Singh Brar's *Beefy's Tune (Dean Blunt Edit)* takes the Babyfather record *"BBF" Hosted by Escrow* (2016) as a vector to think through Black music, diaspora and nation, and the Black arts movement in Britain. He does this by the way of the character Beefy from Franco Rosso's seminal film *Babylon* (1980), as well as through the lost futures of musical duo A. R. Kane. What we get is a foray into the aesthetic potentiality of close listening and the form of historicity that are experienced through race and genre.

Dean Blunt, who heads the Babyfather project, has for a long time been involved in aesthetic ventures that blur the boundaries of art, music and performance, and in many ways has always been imbued with a poetic sensibility, not least in his Tricky-esque MC-ing. What attention to that aesthetic surround does is enable a form of writing, thinking, and feeling that can follow, augment, supplement historically-grounded cultural production. That also means a blurring of music writing, art writing, literary theory and poetics that constitutes a critical writing form that can adequately deal with the multiple questions raised within the confines of a particular cultural or aesthetic object. If compression and tersity must be seen as formal motifs of poetry, then a decompressive thickness can be seen as hallmarks of an essay-form that thinks outside of the bounds of merely the analytical. In reading *Beefy's Tune*, Brar is pushing us to think where the production of culture lays, and in particular to see how vernacular form and theory is embedded in temporal logics of race and aesthetics. Racial-aesthetic irruptions trace these indelible edges; we follow that trace.

– Kashif Sharma-Patel

For Kezia Likinde Rolfe

"I'm not British. I'm not British at all. The British told me that"
Dean Blunt: Everyday is a Lifetime – Microphone Check, NPR,
April 1 2016.

The track hisses into gear with the sound of a party balloon being filled from a gas cylinder.[1] A relatively mundane task, it takes on an air of solemnity due to the carefully plucked accompaniment of digital imitation acoustic guitar. Only a few seconds pass before a voice enters the scene. Pulled from the cultural memory bank, and carrying traces of pitch distortion, the voice is that of a man who proudly boasts "This Makes Me Proud To Be British" whilst an audience applauds. Things remain in this state for almost four minutes: strings fluttering somewhere between bathos and the pathetic, the sample intoning its warped jingoism, and occasional bursts from a gas cylinder, along with a mobile ringtone to add further texture to the action. While it might seem that the intention is to test the listeners limits of the tolerable through the production of a strange, drudging monotony, something more like hypnosis is generated; sonic elements, alien to each other, achieve a kind of cohesion through proximity. The spell though is soon broken with the strafing panic of police sirens. What soon follows is another voice, not sampled this time, more embedded in the action. This new figure, likely the one who has been coordinating the soundscape thus far, complains bitterly about the intrusion from the police. Then

---

[1] With thanks to Larne Abse-Gogarty, Eddie George, Annie Goh, Adam Harper, Paul Rekret and Marie Thompson for reading and commenting on early versions of this.

everything drops out. A crisp, dense bass line eases us from the shock of being suddenly pulled from a trance, and we enter a swaying, nonchalant bounce.

So go the opening moments of the album *"BBF" Hosted by DJ Escrow*, produced by Babyfather, the latest project initiated by Dean Blunt. In many ways the transition from 'Stealth' into 'Greezeblock' – the tracks with which *"BBF"* kicks into motion – is emblematic of the work Blunt has produced since Hype Williams, his breakthrough project with Inga Copeland, and his subsequent solo work. Releases such as *One Nation* (a Hype Williams album recorded in 2011), *Black is Beautiful* (as Dean Blunt and Inga Copeland, 2012), and *The Redeemer* (as Dean Blunt, 2013), alongside innumerable live performances, are arguably determined by three consistencies: a highly wrought artifice combined with an equally wrought authenticity; the burying of clues hinting at decryption that often tend to further obscure; and a sense of embeddedness in a specific cultural landscape but without the need for overt stylistic citations. With 'Stealth'/'Greezeblock' we can hear these consistencies at work in: the light touch use of imitation guitar in combination with what is most likely the sound of nitrous oxide (laughing gas) being pumped into party balloons (a popular, cheap and legal means of achieving a momentary state of intoxication in recent British youth culture); UK Garage / RnB artist Craig David declaring "This Makes Me Proud To Be British" when accepting 'Best RnB Act' and 'Best UK Single' prizes at the 2000 MOBO (Music of Black Origin) Awards. In the footage from the ceremony, we can see David wearing a red sweater with the message "Buy British" stitched across its chest in white; and the presentation of the album as a mixtape recorded during a pirate radio session. Hosted by DJ Escrow, the voice we hear introduced at the close of 'Stealth', the mixtape and pirate radio are central social technologies of Black British music culture.

In this respect, "*BBF*" also sits at the apex of a series of narratives involving the reception of Blunt's work. Switching between irritation and defence, summary dismissal and knee-jerk applause, the discourse surrounding his music tends to run along the following lines: is this an elaborate joke, if so, why are we bothering to give it the time of day? *Or*; is this an elaborate joke, if so can we be let in on the punchline please? The question of Blunt's playing the role of prankster is not all that interesting or important. Instead, what we ought to be asking ourselves is, after listening to "*BBF*", are we on the outside of a tragi-comedy looking in, or are we trapped inside it, desperate to get out? This tragi-comedy, to be clear, goes by the following names: UK plc, Cool Britannia, Blighty, Jerusalem, Three Lions, The Hostile Environment, Take Back Control, A Corner of a Foreign Field That is For Ever England...

Or let me put it like this: to what extent are the elaborate deviations, cloaking devices, orchestrated nonchalance, and seemingly impossible admixtures that are characterised as the definitive qualities of Blunt's music, not only aesthetic decisions but modes of ideological intervention? Is "*BBF*", with its cover image of a Union Jack emblazoned swegway surveying the nauseating gleam of contemporary London – twenty-first century capital of global finance – something like a state of the nation address? Is it an address for the ones who are fucked up enough to believe in the nation? Is it one they'll ever be prepared to listen to? What would such a listening take? Is it possible to be proud to be British and listen to "*BBF*"?

Perhaps the best way to stay with the questions "*BBF*" poses is by affording Blunt the same licence Edouard Glissant gave to Frantz Fanon: diversion. Franco Rosso's 1981 feature film *Babylon* was a political prefiguring of the state of the nation to come. Uncannily grasping the vortex of pressures leading to the great insurrections that began with Brixton in June 1981, flowing over four years through Tottenham, Bristol, Toxteth and Birmingham, *Babylon* is much more than neo-realist cinema as social accounting. Despite having its claims on authenticity questioned at the time for its white director-writing team, and for its apparent production of vulgar images of Black Britons living in the country's internal colonies, *Babylon* has to be considered one of the outstanding achievements of late twentieth century British cinema. The secret to *Babylon* lies in its use of the Ital Lion sound system (played by Mighty Observer) as the structuring pulse of the film. The sound system is the social device ensuring that all the central characters are entangled together. It means that as a unit they can go about making and remaking black aesthetics on a nightly basis in South London. Thus, all of the action which appears to take place away from the sound system is more like its surrounding terrain; the narrative combination of terror, malice, humour and intimacy we see on screen can be understood as flowing back into the speakers as they remodulate social problems and human desires into a thunderous delicateness.

Our concern, though, is not primarily with Ital Lion but one of its emanations. Played by Trevor Laird, Beefy takes up a specific role within the action of *Babylon*. He is presented as a lovable buffoon trapped in the body of a prize-fighter, prone to fits of seemingly irrational violence. Although those within the Ital Lion crew care for him precisely because of these qualities (in that they seek to protect him from his own apparent shortcomings), he is also the constant target of ridicule from rival sounds. The characterisation of Beefy is given even more colour with the gentle, loping trombone sections Dennis Bovell arranged to soundtrack his almost laughable swaggering charm, all carried off in a combination of sweaty gym gear, tattered overcoat, and a giant canine companion.

All of the work done in *Babylon* to present Beefy in one way is a stealth move. In a scene of heightened drama midway through the first third of the film, in which the visceral tensions of Britain's spirit of '45 are put on display, we learn that Beefy is something else. Gathered in their railway arch lockup, where the Ital Lion Crew keep all of their equipment and spend their evenings escaping the ever accumulating brutalities of the day, they are interrupted by a banging at the door. Inevitably it is one of the white neighbours hostile to their sociality, and in fact hostile to the very fact of their existence. The door is eventually opened to a middle-aged white woman, who steps inside:

WOMAN AT LOCK UP: I might have known, I might have known. Look at ya, look at ya, look at ya. Good for nothing. Noisy. Stinking filth. Lazy. You're everywhere. Jungle bunnies. This was a lovely area before you came here. Lovely. [Turns her attention to Ronnie, the Ital Lion crew's white friend] And you, you should be ashamed of yourself you should. You know what you are don't you? You're a traitor to your kith and kin. A traitor.

RONNIE: You're no relative of mine, lady.

WOMAN AT LOCK UP: You fuck off back to your own countries you! Jungle bunnies!

BEEFY: This is my fucking country lady! And it's never been fucking lovely! It's always been a fucking tip! For as long as I can remember! So don't you fucking tell me right!

Despite having to be pulled back by his friends, it would be an error to interpret this as another, albeit more highly charged, instance of Beefy's worst tendencies getting the better of him. Such a line would involve uncritically repeating the view of Beefy as the degraded emblem of the film. Rather, what Beefy delivers here is not a tirade, but a lecture. It is, in fact, a type of public lecture, an educational service. There are very specific reasons as to why the term 'lecture' is the only one that will do.

Whilst on initial viewing it might appear to be an instinctive act driven by righteous rage, Beefy's lecture is a lecture because it is both righteous and much more. Through the combination of intense compression of argument and reorganisation of voice, he displays an intricate mode of theorisation whose basis lies in its stealth. Beefy's lecture involves the precise formalization of stealth as a critical gesture. Throughout the action of the film, Beefy, like his peers in Ital Lion, uses Caribbean patois as his main vehicle for communication. This was an entirely commonplace and practical strategy for many Black British youth; in an environment of a daily hostility patois could be used to gain cohesion by hiding (aurally) in plain sight. The interruption in the lockup however leads Beefy to momentarily switch codes. For the purposes of his lecture, he drops patois – which although a product of the Caribbean, was being made anew in the metropole – and takes up the South London patter which the woman is using as her register of authenticity and authority. This is no act of mimicry. Beefy's switch is so quick and so clean that it's obvious he is equally as sedimented in the local class vernacular. Having flattened the spatial distance between them, Beefy then proceeds to dismantle the ideological assurance the woman feels compelled to perform. Her delusional nostalgia for a picturesque Britain which was convivial before the arrival of the "Good for Nothing. Noisy. Stinking Filth" is skewered by Beefy's corrective that it's always been a "Fucking Tip" – a claim intensified by its delivery in a voice the woman can't fail to recognise as kin to her own.

The idea that Beefy's exchange with the white woman can be understood as a considered act of critical thinking is given greater credence if it is also framed through the institutional venue in which it is delivered. To put it simply: Beefy's lecture functions as such because the sound system already configures itself as a pedagogical instrument. In as much as sound systems are involved in an aesthetic experimentation with sound waves, they are also designed for learning and teaching. This occurs in multiple ways. Organisationally, the sound system crew is a school, whereby junior members are recruited, gain greater responsibility as they observe the work of others, and acquire new skills (whether technical or performative). Alongside this, a sound system is always involved in practices of dialogic knowledge production with its dancefloor. Such analysis – usually issued through the MC/toaster – regularly enters into and rearranges the contours of the sociological, the historical and the political. Evidence of the pedagogical imperative can be found in the proliferation of the moniker 'professor' among dub producers, and the number of sound systems which refer to themselves as universities. Considered in this light, it's easy to see that what Beefy is doing is attempting to teach – as well as admonish – the white woman. He is trying to get her to learn something she appears unable to accept.

By taking together his strategization of stealth and his emergence from an already constituted educational establishment, the fact of Beefy's lecture becomes self-evident. As a lecture on race and nation given at the opening of the 1980s, it also causes trouble. The trouble comes for a lineage of postcolonial thinking concerned with the very same question of Britain as post-imperial problematic, which came into view almost a decade later. When grasped as a lecturer, Beefy has to be placed in the same room as the likes of Homi Bhabha, Avtar Brah, Sara Ahmed and others, and I'm not too sure they'd be all that comfortable finding themselves in such company. This might seem like an outlandish claim to make, but listen closely to the mode of British postcolonial intellectualism Beefy's lecture creates the conditions for, and it begins to fall into place.

Listen first to the correspondence between the way Beefy – in a single moment and with such intricacy – dissolves the terrain from which the woman speaks, and Homi Bhabha's meditation on "minority discourse":

Minority discourse sets the act of emergence in the antagonistic in between of image and sign, the accumulative and the adjunct, presence and proxy. It contests genealogies of 'origin' that lead to claims for cultural supremacy and historical priority. Minority discourse acknowledges the status of national culture – and the people – as a contentious, performative space of the perplexity of the living in the midst of the pedagogical representations of the fullness of life. Now there is no reason to believe that such marks of difference cannot inscribe a 'history' of the people or become the gathering points of political solidarity. They will not, however, celebrate the monumentality of historicist memory, the sociological totality of society, or the homogeneity of cultural experience. (Bhabha, 1994)

Second, listen to Avtar Brah's unpacking of the claims of the native, and its echo of Beefy's weave through the genocidal idea that it is the white woman's privilege – as a Brit – to spew such bile:

In the diaspora space called "England", for example, African-Caribbean, Irish, Asian, Jewish and other diasporas intersect among themselves as well as with the entity constructed as 'Englishness', thoroughly re-inscribing it in the process. Englishness has been formed in the crucible of the internal colonial encounter with Ireland, Scotland and Wales; imperial rivalries with other European countries; and imperial conquests abroad. In the post-war period this Englishness is continually reconstituted via a multitude of border crossings in and through other diasporic formations. These border crossings are territorial, political, economic, cultural and psychological. This Englishness is a new ensemble that both appropriates and is in turn appropriated by British-based African-Caribbean-ness, Asian-ness, Irishness and so on. Each of these formations has its own specificity, but it is an ever-changing specificity that adds to as well as imbues elements of the other. What I am proposing here is that border crossings do not occur only across the dominant / dominated dichotomy, but that, equally, there is traffic within cultural formations of the subordinated groups, and that these journeys are not *always* mediated through the dominant cultures. (Brah, 1996)

Finally, in as much as Sara Ahmed is understood as a student of Brah's, it's really the case that she is a student of Beefy's own strange encounter, when he melts his way through the flimsy authority the white woman uses as her weapon, sneaks – figuratively – up to her ear, and whispers: *the closer I get to you / the more you make me see:*

Narratives which construct 'the strange culture' as their object (distance), are also contaminated by that very object (proximity). Colonial encounters do not just involve a transition from distance to proximity: they involve, at one and the same time, social and spatial relations of distance and proximity. Others become strangers (the ones who are distant), only through coming *too close to home*, that is, through the proximity of the encounter, or 'facing', itself. (Ahmed, 2000)

Beefy is the originator of a postcolonial style that never lays claim to him and likely doesn't wish to either. Whatever the specificities of Bhabha, Brah and Ahmed's thinking (and they are only exemplars, not the sole occurrences), Beefy had already named, theorised and performed those dynamics deep in the recesses of a South London lock-up recast as a public lecture theatre. They seem so close, yet there are entire land masses between them.

Beefy's lecture, then, is one of the most pivotal moments in this critical piece of British cinema. It is so not simply because of its excoriating accuracy, but also due to the way he conceptually orchestrates it as a stealth manoeuvre, an apparently sudden transformation which, for a moment, takes him uncomfortably close to the home (and theoretical school) that doesn't want him. This tells us something of the nature of Beefy's tune. It might be that his outward appearance is the best defence he can come up with for the burden he carries, a burden we can understand as the wages of black labour: *We are here because you were there, and over there we built here*. But Beefy is able to bear this burden, because he's not just Beefy, he's also Ital Lion, and the Lion is on a mission to protect its people, but it's also on a mission to save and teach those who believe his people don't belong here. How does the Ital Lion protect, teach and save? By night, after night, using its sensory poetics to transform the interior world of this tip into something more bearable, more righteous: a university of dub.

Trevor Laird's heroic realisation of Beefy was not a solo affair in early 1980s Britain. His lecture can be placed within a revelatory stream of dissident black professing all working on the same postcolonial burden. We can hear something of Beefy's tune in Linton Kwesi Johnson's performance of 'Inglan is a Bitch' on the Old Grey Whistle Test. And Smiley Culture's 'Cockney Translation' could be thought of as a cover of a Beefy original. Therefore, in so far as Laird's Beefy forms part of a pedagogical assemblage in the pressure cooker of Thatcherite Britain, I want to propose that Dean Blunt also moves in this stream, as its extension and repurposing. Whereas with LKJ and Smiley, the intricacies of Britain as a tip are held across a knife-edge of wit and rebellion, what places Blunt within the trajectory opened up by Beefy are the qualities of the cloaking device, of the sudden reveal of a truth too uncomfortable to properly register so that most of the time it has to be hidden behind a veneer of tom-foolery. To my ears at least, 'Stealth' sounds like an edit of Beefy's lecture done thirty-seven years down the line. Blunt, though, is not paying homage. Rather, he recognises that the historical distance between 1980 and 2016 has been mistaken for progress. Both he (with "*BBF*") and Beefy (in *Babylon*) are able to use the momentary code switch, the sleight of the mask, to construct black art and thought (in all its accuracy, brutality and beauty) in the face of a nationalism that keeps on enforcing its genocidal myths.

One of the easiest things to say about Dean Blunt is that his music lacks seriousness. In fact, one of the most common laudatory assessments his work is given is that it is a labyrinthine orchestration of the absence of seriousness delivered with a veneer of solemnity. Blunt is considered something of a performance art prankster, skilled in using the most affectless deadpan to build layer after layer of in-jokes, nods, winks and sly asides. This is thought to be the cause of the compulsion-repulsion effect that surrounds him. The latter view is based on the notion that his schtick is nothing more than an elaborate method of accumulating social and cultural capital which, at best, exposes the corrupting effects of the contemporary conjoining of art and experimental music. The former favours Blunt precisely for his exposure of the flows of capital within arenas which purport to support and generate aesthetic (as well as social) radicalism. Early on in the development of such a hermeneutic, Kodwo Eshun signalled that, perhaps, there might be a rush to judgment on both sides. His 2011 review of a set of Hype Williams releases gives conceptual purchase to a guiding imperative of their sound. What he calls Hype Williams' "insistent inappropriateness" shapes the way in which on albums such as *One Nation* (2011) and *Find Out What Happens When People Stop Being Polite, And Start Gettin' Reel* (2010), they use Wiley lyrics as titles for tracks which never go close to the soundworld of Grime, whilst also covering Sade and George Michael, without fulling arriving at the original song. Populated with evasions of this type, as well as accumulated clouds of sound which skirt the edges of identifiable styles, Eshun hears in their work "moments of inspired incongruity". The key to his review though lies in the way Eshun is able to transfer an assessment of the internal form and content of a Hype Williams record, into an account of the inappropriateness that imbued their outward facing dynamics:

What if the often remarked upon knowingness of the duo was designed to protect the right to fabricate songs that didn't know where they were going?

One reason why people love, hate and love to hate Hype Williams is that their disinterest in digital professionalism translates into a refusal to grow up and treat music as a serious profession for serious people. The duo's attitude remains one of allusive insolence, insistent infantilism and sustained self-absorption, nurtured by an exorbitant sense of entitlement....

The heteronyms, the fake back stories, the aggravating YouTube video loops, the misleading song titles, the obstinate, obstreperous, obnoxious attitude: all of it seems to operate as a series of in-jokes designed to project a forcefield of irritation capable of deflecting the attention of anyone naive enough to enquire as to its purpose. (Eshun, 2011)

Eshun was not alone in picking up on these tendencies in Hype Williams. Marie Thompson also heard a deliberate aesthetic strategy in their use of irritation and subterfuge:

> In Hype Williams, the signature noise of multiple mediums can be heard: the hazy, lo-fi effect of their recordings is mostly generated by analogue and digital media noise. Tracks are undercut by hiss, while tape warbles create distinctive pitch bends....Many of their samples sound as if they have been ripped from YouTube videos: the audio artefacts and effects that arise with lossy digital compression....feature frequently. Just as it is impossible to tell what is fact from fiction about Hype Williams, the saturation of their music with noise makes it difficult to discern what sounds are coming from where – what is 'live' and what is sampled....
>
> Hype Williams production style both generates and disrupts a sonic fantasy: their music sounds as if it could be played from 'lo-fi' media, and yet repeatedly reveals this to be an illusion – it is simultaneously too noisy and not noisy enough to be true. (Thompson, 2017)

Both Eshun and Thompson locked onto a dimension of the Hype Williams project which, at the time, went relatively unnoticed, and I would suggest, continues to determine Blunt's work. Which is to say that in Blunt's sound we hear the use of evasion and mystification, the generation and disruption of fantasy, to such an extent that the resulting irritation is deployed to carefully slip into the music a piercing and astute slice of honesty. It's possible to spot the myriad ways in which Blunt has made use of this strategy once one becomes attuned to it. With *Black Metal* he reverses the polarities of Hype Williams by foregrounding the solo guitar and untreated vocals (as mechanisms designed to leave the artist exposed), to weave intricate songs which appear to tell the story of a breakup between a roadman and his 'girl'. The live show *Free Jazz*, performed at London's premier avant-garde / experimental music venue Cafe Oto, was conducted in pitch darkness and interspersed with monologue poems sneering at Kim Gordon, yet it explored rather than mocked a historical monument of late twentieth century black aesthetics. *XTASY (EDDIE PEAKE WET DREEM)*, a work secreted on YouTube sees Blunt locate a granular admixture of terror and joy spread across the surfaces of D'Angelo's generously seductive performance for his 'Untitled (How Does it Feel)' video. "*BBF*" then, forms part of Blunt's development of a mode initially conceived for Hype Williams. The album is a stand out work for Blunt, and is able to function as an ideological intervention, because the tactics of evasion combined with irritation in the service of a coded integrity, is remodelled, given a voice and given a name. With "*BBF*" a previously employed aesthetic strategy is transformed into a character.

Within the context of the album presented as mixtape, DJ Escrow ('played' by poet James Massiah) is our host. He guides the listener through proceedings and the conceit is that he is the one selecting the music. In terms of getting to grips with the direction of travel for the album, Escrow is its unexpected star, taking the focus of attention away from Blunt, who besides producing, appears at points to vocalise in his signature detached monotone that hints at heartbreak. As both host and lead character, Escrow serves as a fulcrum, one through which the ethos of the album is established, before it is eroded to open up a secondary, more complex rhythm for the whole work. Initially, we listen to Escrow as a caricature, a ludic figure designed to partly send up, partly nod to, the vocal toolkit of the pirate radio host. In this sense, Escrow's chatter becomes increasingly absurd because it appears to be incongruous with the dissonant abstraction of Blunt's productions. As the album proceeds, Escrow is still there front and centre, holding court, giving shout outs, noting postcodes. And it becomes difficult to smirk at him, as his commentaries become increasingly reflective, musing on the political geography of London, the myriad modes of identification for diasporans, and the fraught sociality of the dancefloor. As Angus Finlayson notes of the albums central figure:

You grow to like him, which is a strange thing to say about such a cryptic character on such a knotty album. It helps that he shows his vulnerable side. (Finlayson, 2016)

Not only do we grow to like Escrow, but we soon realise that the 'humour' engendered by the supposed discrepancy between him and the soundscape, was in truth derived from our own prejudices blocking our ears to the intent of the album. In fact, rather than a deliciously inappropriate friction, Escrow sits perfectly within Blunt's productions, and as opposed to listening for evasion, we are simply required to take him, and the music, at its word. Be sincere.

Escrow's sincerity – which we can take to be an amplified version of Blunt's own – shines through on 'PROLIFIC DAEMONS'. The three-minute track becomes critical to comprehending what is at stake in "*BBF*" because it is the point at which we, as an audience, undergo a transformation from those listening with a knowing cynicism which allows us to believe we are in some way in on the joke, to an audience who realise the jokes been on them all along. On initial encounter 'PROLIFIC DAEMONS' is organised around an incompatibility. The musical components of the track are dominated by a score resembling the screaming metal of a jet engine roar. The intensity of the soundscape is relentless, never dropping or deviating in its measure, soaking the piece in ear-damaging distortion. The performative centre of 'PROLIFIC DAEMONS' is Escrow. He is braided through the roar, gleefully fulfilling his role as host. He calls out to all the nine-to-five office workers who are really from the roads, but hiding in the drudgery of the corporate world, asking them to join him in the joyous reverie of his selection. Escrow then proceeds to take messages and dropped calls on the station mobile, the only means pirates have of knowing if anyone is locked into their signal. Finally, he delivers a thirty second sermon, denouncing those who – by fighting amongst themselves – disrupt the leisure time and minor entrepreneurship of people trying to organise parties. For some there might be a deliberate, maze-like, suggestiveness to 'PROLIFIC DAEMONS'. It could be the case that Blunt has, after the fact, edited Escrow's broadcast and inserted the Noise soundtrack, thus sending up the conventions of the mixtape format. Or Escrow might be blissfully unaware that what he is playing registers as Noise, making the broadcast a failed one because a host worthy of the name would never subject their listeners to such an extreme indulgence. There is even the possibility that both Blunt and Escrow are in on the joke together, and it is their express aim to engineer such failure.

Neither of these possible assessments of 'PROLIFIC DAEMONS' are satisfactory because they do not take Blunt or Escrow seriously, instead relying on the idea that the album is conditioned by an attitude of mockery. Daniel Neofetou, in his review of "*BBF*", zeroes in on the problems 'PROLIFIC DAEMONS' raises concerning listenership, intent and interpretation:

"*BBF*" is a pastiche in the very literal sense that it takes the form of a mixtape but is being released on CD and LP. And its press release is decidedly sardonic, referring to the albums lead single 'Meditation' as a 'street classic', and featuring a lengthy fabricated quote attributed to actor Idris Elba waxing lyrical about the record. *There's nothing fake about the record itself, however, and any interpretations of irony will largely be rooted in the audiences prejudices about who and what certain styles of music are for....*

And on the noise track 'PROLIFIC DAEMONS', DJ Escrow shouts out 'all my Gs making Ps legit', urging listeners to play the track loud even if they work in an office so that their bosses know that they're 'from the roads'. *Yet beyond the ostensible humour of these juxtapositions are the questions of why noise music should be the preserve of the (white) avant-garde, and conversely why a black artist should negate the influence of their formative music if they're welcomed into this scene.* (Neofetou, 2016, emphasis added)

For Neofetou, what Dean Blunt is involved in is not simply making music qua music, but producing music that instigates (racial) trouble for the listener. What a track such as 'PROLIFIC DAEMONS' does is expose a series of assumptions about musical categorisation under the heading 'avant-garde' or even 'experimental' that are never limited to the musical (whilst recognising how contested both terms are historically and when used in relation to the scene in which Blunt operates). Instead, for Neofetou, Blunt is realising a project which shows that the avant-garde or experimental is far from a liberated zone of limitless reconfiguration. The uncomfortable truth is that the very basis for the avant-garde/experimental claim upon musical freedom requires some border police. Neofetou is not alone in making such an argument. Fred Moten also draws out the violent geographical dimensions of the racial problematic of musical avant-gardes:

The idea of the avant-garde is embedded in a theory of history. This is to say that a particular geographical ideology, a geographical-racial or racist unconscious, marks and is the problematic out of which or against the backdrop of which the idea of the avant-garde emerges....

What I've been specifically interested in here is how the idea of a black avant-garde exists, as it were, oxymoronically – as if black, on the one hand, and avant-garde, on the other hand, each depends for its coherence upon the exclusion of the other. (Moten, 2003)

What we have with Neofetou and Moten is an identification

of the ways in which all too easy assertions of aesthetic experimentation are haunted by the xenophobic. There is a way in which the process of constructing a musical category according to relative degrees of 'freedom' can very quickly shift into thinking a music as definitive of a culture, and thus qualitatively reflective of a people, all of which lends itself to an unscripted but undeniably persistent notion that a particular musical freedom has a 'home' adequate to its (racial) sensibilities. The outcome is that if a musical culture shifts, bleeds, spreads, migrates and dissipates into alien territory, then the results are considered at best novel, at times absurd, but in most cases fatal. Or to put it plainly: fuck off back to your own (musical) country.

Blunt himself is fully aware of the problem of xenophobia which shadows the construction of genre, and therefore audience, in musical claims upon the experimental:

I think genre terms are really connected, at least for me, to race and boundaries, and I think if you've been – if you've experienced any kind of isolation or boundaries, you definitely treat genres in the same way that you feel about race, I think, naturally, for me. So I don't think about genres that consciously. It's not something that I think of. It's just that I consume, and – I get really put off by people that are too conscious of genre. I find that people who are too conscious of genre usually are way too conscious of race and way too conscious of shit that I also get irritated by. And so I usually avoid – don't really fuck with them, in general, or make music with them, or whatever. (NPR, 2016)

Clearly there is a way in which the racial policing of the avant-garde and the experimental corresponds with the racial policing of the nation. The violent assembly of home and belonging is as much an aesthetic endeavour as it is a policy issue. Xenophobia is an experimental art thing in the same way as it is a passport thing. But what Blunt makes apparent through "*BBF*" – Neofetou and Moten point to this too – is that simple inclusion is not the answer. It is not about the diversification of the avant-garde and the experimental as a salve for the brutal imposition of the nation. We are not talking about demands to be seen, heard or recognised. Instead, what "*BBF*" does is collapse the racial border between the avant-garde and black social music, not by sitting in the ambivalence of the 'between', but by stealthily ignoring it altogether. Through this sonic programming of stealth, Blunt flushes out the xenophobic aestheticisation of the experimental, and as I will go onto show, exposes an internalised policing of black music as necessarily anti-avant-gardist.

The nature of the ideological intervention being made with "*BBF*", the tone of Blunt's state of the (musical) nation address, is coming into view now. With its explicit presentation as a mixtape, the depth of characterisation given to Escrow, and the loop of Craig David's moment of pride as an absurd long lost memory, "*BBF*" is joining an ongoing debate about the valences of the aesthetic, social, cultural and political claims upon blackness made by those unlucky enough to be born in – or tethered to – Britain. At the very same time, and through its unsettling deployment of sonic elements, *"BBF"* is asking the question: What is the purpose of musical (as a segment of a general aesthetic) categorisation? Why does the categorisation of music function so similarly to the modes of categorisation used to racially determine the nation? Why does the free movement of music across the border of genre raise such violent consternation?' In what sense is listening, and its resulting construction of an audience, an activity that can easily lend itself to a xenophobic disposition?

In the same way that Blunt's *"BBF"* is moving in the stream opened up by Trevor Laird's Beefy in 1980, the album is also resuscitating the problem-space which determined another project later in the decade. The Black British Arts Movement (which could in some sense be understood as the programatisation of Beefy's lecture) was forged in the ever-intensifying echoes after the great insurrections of the early 1980s. Often invoked through the name-checking of major artists (Sonia Boyce, Lubaina Himid, Eddie Chambers, Rasheed Araeen), Black British Arts sustained a number of debates over the nature of the project and several overlapping, contesting, iterations. For some, the defining feature of Black British Arts was that it represented a break from the international modernism of an earlier anti-colonial realisation of visual art, towards a more nationally conscious black aesthetic. In turn, this lead to an ongoing discussion – a tension, even – over the relation between militancy and theory, politics and abstraction. Another understanding of Black British Arts which developed over its formation centred on refusing to conceive of the art as a transcendental register of a new aesthetic regime, and instead seeing it as a deluge of collectively realised practices which signalled the coming of a monumental structural shift in British society. Taken as a whole, what unified the various trajectories of the Black British Arts Movement was the task of assembling a black aesthetics in the setting of an inoperable former empire and the racial enclosure of the nation state.

The specific moment in Black British Arts that I want to single out for the purpose of thinking "*BBF*" is a series of exchanges that took place between Kobena Mercer and Paul Gilroy. Stimulated by the arrival of New Black Cinema (exemplified by its three leading projects Sankofa, Ceddo and Black Audio Film Collective), Mercer and Gilroy were not so much discussing the merits of a set of films as films, but pushing a debate on black aesthetics which centred on the politics of form and audience, all within a context in which the relation between blackness and the (post-imperial) nation was already a battleground.

To summarise, Gilroy put into question the validity of films such a *Handsworth Songs* and *Passion of Remembrance* because of the problems he saw issuing from their avant-gardism. Gilroy's line was that the embrace of European experimentalism and high theory was not a problem for the films in and of themselves, but it did mean that the economic circuits of the international arts became the primary orientation for these works and the artists who made them:

Black filmic production in particular is tightly shackled into a relationship of dependency on overground cultural institutions which are both capital – and labour – intensive. When, then, is it becoming illegitimate to ask how different

are the black audiences for these films from the white? This can be a polite way of formulating a deeper and more shocking question: namely, is there *any* black audience for some of these most highly prized productions of the black arts movement? Is there a non-literate, black, working or non-working class audience eagerly anticipating these particular cultural products? Have 'our' film-makers given up the pursuit of an audience outside the immediate, symbolic formation in which black 'filmic texts' originate? (Gilroy, 1993)

Using the charge that the New Black Cinema represented an abdication of social and political responsibility precisely because of its avant-garde appearance, Gilroy argued that the core imperative for a Black British Arts should be a grounding in the vernacular. Leaning heavily on his hero Amiri Baraka, he called for a "populist modernism" in Black British Arts:

The most basic formal expression of this development can be recognised in the need to articulate a positive core of aesthetic modernism in resolutely vernacular formats. This is something which is not confined to cinema alone, although it marks some of the films that we have looked at. It is shared by a wide range of different cultural expression. Toni Morrison's *Beloved* for example, seems to me to be doing something of this type. Lenny Henry's recent performances in the character of Delbert Wilkins – in the most recent series of *The Lenny Henry Show* – seem to be doing something similar as well. Now, the term populist modernism shouldn't just be used as a way of marking out those adventuresome black borrowings from and adaptation of a preformed Western canon. It can also be applied where black artists and thinkers have attempted to construct their own distinct sense of modernism that reflects their peculiar relationship to modernity. We have had very intense and particular experiences of the modern world, experiences which evade capture by concepts like 'communicative ethics' and require a special gloss on terms like justice and reason. We also need to emphasise that blacks have their own traditions of inquiry into the politics of representation. These need to be reactivated, resuscitated, and drawn on, explicitly rather than implicitly. In particular, they need to be recovered and brought into debates which are just beginning in British cultural politics. (Gilroy, 1988)

Kobena Mercer sought to defend New Black Cinema as a vital intensification of the political aesthetics of blackness into terrain which was risky, but necessary. Thus, his response to Gilroy's stress upon the vernacular was to frame it as an attempt to close off possibilities for enriching the scope and dimension of Black British Art. Mercer achieved this in two ways, first by claiming Gilroy's use of class reflected a moralism rather than modernism, and as such it was a class analysis which lacked a grounding in the material:

There is something wrong with this picture – for although the issue of audience is certainly important, the shape of the question is closed rather than open (it is implicit the answers are already known in advance). Moreover, in assuming that authorial intentions determine the socioeconomic composition of audiences, the argument risks the return of certain class reductionism, whereby the value is judged by the race/class composition of the audience for which it was intended. (Mercer, 1994)

Secondly, he suggested that the trope of populist modernism reproduces the very modes of racial authenticity and nationalism which Gilroy himself had spent his career virulently attacking:

In my view, this item of unfinished business from the past makes an unbidden return in 'populist modernism' when it is implied that, to put it crudely, black artists who choose to work in vernacular forms, addressing a popular audience, are artists who produce art worth arguing over; while black artists whose work is taken up by white elites, on the other hand, by virtue of their choice of medium, have no basis of belonging in the black communities, and hence produce nothing work talking about. (Mercer, 1994)

The debate between Gilroy and Mercer serves to illuminate a specific node within the broader problem space of Black British Arts. This was a node which explicitly linked the question of race and nation (how to make Black Art in Britain) to what were framed as tensions between the popular or vernacular (which Gilroy reads as equivalent to blackness) and avant-garde experimentalism (seen by him, at the very least, as not black). Thus, their exchange in the late 1980s carries strong echoes of the very problematic "*BBF*" appears to occupy in 2017, and indicates how the album functions as an ideological intervention. "*BBF*" shows us that the questions being hammered out so publicly over thirty years ago are still alive in our present. There is an elephant in the room though, and in a sense it points to a major failure of the Black British Arts project. "*BBF*" is not a piece of cinema, so to place it within the remit of a debate about black innovation in such a form is somewhat flawed. However, by folding "*BBF*" back into a discourse about New Black Cinema, we can illuminate how black music never received an adequate hearing in the crucible of Black British Arts. Music was not – aesthetically or conceptually – considered a central part of the deluge of works in this decade.

To make such a claim stick, we need to pay closer attention to the resources of Gilroy's argument as it has been presented above. When he was laying out the case for black populist modernism, it was not really Toni Morrison, Lenny Henry or even James Baldwin who were the primary drivers of the thesis. These names are covers for the real resources of his argument: Curtis Mayfield, Bob Marley, Rico Rodriguez, Rakim and Soul II Soul. Stepping back from the specificities of the exchange with Mercer and looking across his body of work, for Gilroy populist modernism was always a sonic project first and foremost, and his insistence upon the vernacular in a debate about cinema was arguably determined by his understanding of the sound system: a black working-class sonic technology imported into Britain from the Caribbean. Within the context of Black British Arts, Gilroy was the only intellectual seriously engaged with and making a consistent case for what we could call Black British Sonic Arts. In his contributions to *The Empire Strikes Back*, the penultimate chapter of *There Ain't No Black in the Union*

Jack, and throughout *The Black Atlantic*, Gilroy pointed to the real-time assembly of sonic culture, its incessant making, unmaking and remaking of the lower frequencies of the political, all mediated by the irreducible social dialogics – the inherently formal exchangeability – of black diasporic music. These concerns were rarely, if ever, taken up by any of the leading practitioners or thinkers in Black British Arts.

But if understood as a case for the music, rather than a case for an alternative New Black Cinema, then his exchange with Mercer simultaneously exposes Gilroy's severe critical curtailing of the possibilities for black music as a central part of Black British Arts, and for Black British Music itself. By working on the basis that music is the unacknowledged referent in the responses to Mercer, then Gilroy is quite correct in suggesting music has greater institutional autonomy than cinema. Yet Gilroy is also insistent that this idealised vernacular sense of the music is *de facto* hostile to and incompatible with anything that looks, sounds or smells like his prefigured idea of the avant-garde. What makes Gilroy's argument equal parts elusive and troubling is that he knows Mercer doesn't have the analytical equipment to adequately think black music (and is this exemplary of a wider failure of Black British Arts when it comes to the sonic). Having said that, Mercer's response is still pertinent. Gilroy *is* generating a class reductionism and he *is* policing the borders of authenticity, not those of black cinema but of black music.

All of these flaws, failings and aporias of both Black British Arts and Gilroy's insistence on the ideological opposition between the vernacular and the experimental in black music, only come into view if filtered retrospectively through the provocations of Blunt's "*BBF*". The fact it is a musical undertaking means "*BBF*" reawakens the old sonic ghosts in the machinery of Black British Arts, precisely when the project begins to return to the cultural consciousness. "*BBF*" is designed according to the rubrics of the social technology of the pirate mixtape, a resolutely vernacular mode of experimentation in Black British aesthetics derived from the sound system, which in itself has issued forth style after mutated style of sonic culture. The album's formal mode of attack is to deploy techniques normally registered as experimental or avant-garde to work towards their own dissolution, not through that old process of *aufhebung*, but by swamping the system with alien population (as represented by Escrow). The effect is not the sort of vanquishing of a disloyal black avant-garde by means of the vernacular (as Gilroy imagined it), and neither is it the infinitely differentiated blackness as a kind of dinner party game for an elite professoriate (see Mercer). Instead, if we listen closely to Blunt, he lets us know "*BBF*" is drawing on the residues of another, more obscured, musical project which flourished precisely in the cracks of Black British Art in the late 1980s:

You have to understand, Hackney is really cut off from London in a very specific way. *AR Kane are from Hackney.* It's almost like Staten Island. Apart from street bullshit, you didn't leave the borough, so this borough is my city. And it is romantic. It's as pretty as any other part of the world.....
Hackney is a place that's either full of possibilities that aren't real, that never really existed and diversity that never really existed, or just generally a way brighter world that never

really existed living here. And that weight is what I mean when I talk about the weight of living here. It's kind of dreams and ideals you had of the world beyond it. That's what here is. It's good when you come back older, because then you can just experience it for the dream. (Keenan, 2014, emphasis added)

Blunt's album (and this could possibly apply to all his output) functions as a kind of love letter to the blackness of Hackney, which in turn is a romance, a dream of Black Britain (and thus Black British Music) that did exist but was never permitted to be realised. "*BBF*" operates in this dream state not only through its singular incorporation of the moods of pirate radio, which traversed the landscape of the borough, but also because Blunt knows that to enter into the black romance of Hackney (as a cipher for a Black British music that never left its confines or was never heard in Black British Arts), you also need to able to hold AR Kane within such a field. Blunt's momentary appeal to AR Kane is perhaps the closest to a full reveal that appears through his reams of deceptive – sometimes even antagonistic – interviews. They become one of the sharpest lenses through which to think the atmospheres he creates on "*BBF*" and across his discography. The duo of Alex Ayuli and Rudy Tambala, two childhood friends of Nigerian and Malawian migrants who settled in the borough, had – as AR Kane – from 1986 to 1994 taken on the task of detourning the settled racial terrain of experimental British pop music. Initially – and unsurprisingly – miscast as a black derivative of a seemingly white Shoegaze / Noise aesthetic defined by The Jesus and

Mary Chain and My Bloody Valentine, the sheer originality of the AR Kane sound meant they bled out any lazy colour coded assumptions. Instead Ayuli and Tambala would insist that as far as they had any influences, they came only from electric Miles, the cavernous materiality of dub, and Sun Ra's recoding of the synthesiser. What resulted was not a music which cited these totems of black sonic experimentation in any noticeable way, but rather generated what they called "dream pop", which took these touchstone sensibilities into an alternate terrain. The mood of AR Kane's dream pop on records such as 69, "*i*" and *Lolita* displayed an unsettling ability to traverse glistening liquidity and almost sadistic aggression. The resonance with Blunt is clear to the extent that a track such as 'And I Say' could easily be included as part of an after the fact Hype Williams file drop, and the same goes for 'in a circle' and his early solo work. This is why the Hackney convergence is no joke. Listen to Tambala describe how he and Ayuli constructed an alternative aesthetic imperative for Black British Art out east, whilst Gilroy and Mercer were trading blows over in the ICA:

We were aware of the necessity of 'flaws' in music....these flaws are discontinuities that act as tiny fissures, allowing the dim and distant, diffused gem light of pre-creation to slip thru – it is this that the music existed for – a signpost, a reminder, a note. BTW, that's a theory. We called it 'Kaning' the music. So-called perfect music, whatever genre – aims to remove these flaws, to have a true and complete, finished thing. The flaws leave a space, where the listener can still add something of her own, where she can sit and be. AR Kane is one person, comprised of two people. We never had enough individual Kane to make flawed music individually; it needed the two of us, working as closely as lovers, in complete trust and proximity. It is telepathy, the children's marbles dropping from our mouths, laughing, then more marbles, and coloured sticks and rubber bands. (Kulkarni, 2012)

To tighten (but in no sense clarify) the swirl of associations orbiting here, we need to go back to Dennis Bovell. The composer of Beefy's Tune becomes a vital figure in the dream of Black British Music shared by Blunt and AR Kane. This is because Bovell also extolled the capacities of error as the structural principle of experimentation in dub. This sensibility for the mistake that dub installed was something Bovell spent the 1980s diffusing across the landscape of black music as a way of constantly inventing new shapes for it. We can hear the mistake elsewhere on the soundtrack to *Babylon* via the sharpened horn dread flexibility of 'Warrior Charge'; it's also present as the sizzling transposition of Janet Kay's voice into signal on 'Silly Games'; and it comes as no surprise that The Slits and The Pop Group came knocking at his door when they knew error was what they were looking for.

What if Dean Blunt too, is making music organised around the necessity of its own flaws? What if he – like AR Kane – needs to invent a new entity (comprised of himself, DJ Escrow, and Gasman, the three members of Babyfather) in order to make music with enough mistakes? As was the case with Dennis Bovell, what if the activation of error is the basis of Blunt's musical, categorical, cultural and therefore ideological intervention into the racial-aesthetic logic of the nation? The path from mistake to error to flaw to transgression rides along the violently policed border between being proud to be British and knowing Britain doesn't want you. Such was the score for Beefy's Tune. AR Kane heard it a decade later and turned it into dream pop. Maybe, with Blunt's "*BBF*" we are locked into its latest pirate transmission.

Bibliography

Sara Ahmed, *Embodied Others: Strange Encounters in Post-Coloniality* (Routledge, 2000).

Homi Bhabha, *The Location of Culture* (Routledge, 1994).

Avtar Brah, *Cartographies of Diaspora: Contesting Identities* (Routledge, 1996).

Eden Charles, "No War in This Babylon", in *Race Today Review* (January 1981).

Kodwo Eshun, "One Nation / Kelly Price W8 Gain EP Vol II" in *The Wire* (329, July 2011).

Angus Finlayson, "Babyfather – BBF Hosted by DJ Escrow", *Resident Advisor* (April 1, 2016). https://www.residentadvisor.net/reviews/18815

Paul Gilroy, "Cruciality and the frog's perspective: An agenda of difficulties for the black arts movement in Britain", *Small Acts: Thoughts on the Politics of Black Cultures* (Serpent's Tail, 1993).

Paul Gilroy, "Nothing But Sweat Inside My Hand" Diaspora Aesthetics and Black Arts in Britain", in Kobena Mercer (ed), *Black Film, British Cinema* (ICA Documents 7, 1988).

Vivien Goldman, "The Brethren in Babylon" in *Timeout* (November 7 1980).

David Kennan, "To Live and Die in E5" in *The Wire* (367, September 2014).

Neil Kulkarni, "The Future Came and Went: A.R Kane Interviewed", *The Quietus* (October 11, 2012). https://thequietus.com/articles/10306-a-r-kane-interview

Kobena Mercer, "Black Art and the Burden of Representation", *Welcome to the Jungle: New Positions in Black Cultural Studies* (Routledge, 1994).

Fred Moten, *In the Break: The Aesthetics of the Black Radical Tradition* (University of Minnesota Press, 2003).

Daniel Neofetou, "BBF Hosted by DJ Escrow" in *The Wire* (386, April 2016).

NPR - Microphone Check, "Dean Blunt: Everyday is a Lifetime", (April 1, 2016). https://www.npr.org/sections/microphonecheck/2016/04/01/472637838/dean-blunt-everyday-is-a-lifetime?t=1576149720616

Ian Penman, "Dennis Bovell: Dub Wares", *Vital Signs: Music, Movies and Other Manias* (Serpent's Tail, 1998).

Marie Thompson, *Beyond Unwanted Sound: Noise, Affect and Aesthetic Moralism* (Bloomsbury, 2017).

Discography / Filmography

Babyfather, *"BBF" Hosted by DJ Escrow* (Hyperdub, 2016).

Dean Blunt, *Black Metal* (Rough Trade, 2014).

Dean Blunt, "FREE JAZZ LIVE AT CAFE OTO". https://www.youtube.com/watch?v=MMoj1autQnA

Dean Blunt, "XTASY (EDDIE PEAKE WET DREEM)". https://www.youtube.com/watch?v=PBxnzcoHzow

Smiley Culture, *Cockney Translation* (Fashion Records, 1984).

Linton Kwesi Johnson, "Inglan is a Bitch". https://www.youtube.com/watch?v=Zq9OpJYck7Y

AR Kane, 69 (Rough Trade, 1988).

AR Kane, "*i*" (Rough Trade, 1989).

AR Kane, *Lolita* (4AD, 1987).

Janet Kay, *Silly Games* (Arawak, 1977).

Franco Rosso, *Babylon* (National Film Finance Corporation, 1980).

The Slits, *Cut* (Island Records, 1979).

Various, *Babylon: The Original Soundtrack*, (Chrysalis, 1980).

Hype Williams, *Find Out What Happens Stop Being Polite, And Start Gettin Reel* (De Stijl, 2010).

Hype Williams, *One Nation* (Hippos in Tanks, 2011).

The Pop Group, *Y* (Radar Records, 1979).